The Depths of Atonement: Understanding God's Plan for Redemption

By LD Lewis

Introduction

The doctrine of atonement lies at the heart of Christian faith and theology, presenting God's ultimate solution to humanity's greatest problem—sin. It is through atonement that a holy and righteous God reconciles sinful, fallen humanity to Himself, restoring what was broken and healing what was lost. The word "atonement," often defined as "at-one-ment," conveys the profound truth of reconciliation, a unity brought about only through the sacrificial work of Jesus Christ.

From the first pages of Genesis to the final visions in Revelation, the theme of atonement weaves through Scripture as a scarlet thread, binding God's plan of redemption into one cohesive story. In the Old Testament, the sacrificial system established by God pointed forward to the ultimate, perfect sacrifice of Jesus Christ, who fulfilled and transcended all that the Law foreshadowed. In the New Testament, the cross stands as the pivotal moment in history where justice and mercy meet, where sin is dealt with, and where love triumphs over death.

This book seeks to delve into the depths of the atonement, exploring its theological, biblical, and even scientific dimensions. Drawing from the timeless wisdom of the King James Bible, the theological clarity of Myer Pearlman's *Knowing the Doctrines of the Bible*, the fascinating insights of M.R. DeHaan's *The Chemistry of the Blood*, and the linguistic precision of *Strong's Concordance*, we will uncover the multifaceted beauty of God's redemptive plan. This study is not merely academic; it is deeply practical and transformative. Understanding the atonement compels us to worship, live holy lives, and share the good news with a world in desperate need of reconciliation.

As you journey through the pages of this book, you will be challenged to see the depths of your own sin and the heights of God's grace. You will discover the life-giving power of the blood of Christ and be drawn into the wonder of what it means to be "at one" with God. May this study deepen your faith, enrich your understanding, and inspire you to live in the light of the cross.

Chapter 1: The Need for Atonement

1.1 Defining Atonement

The term "atonement" originates from the Hebrew word **kaphar** (Strong's H3722), which means "to cover, purge, make reconciliation." It signifies a covering for sin that satisfies the demands of divine justice and restores fellowship between God and man. In the Old Testament, this covering was symbolized through the blood of sacrificial animals. In the New Testament, it is fulfilled in the sacrificial death of Jesus Christ, whose blood does not merely cover sin but removes it completely (Hebrews 10:4, John 1:29).

Atonement answers the greatest question of all: How can a holy God, who is just and perfect, restore sinful humanity to Himself without compromising His righteousness? The answer is found in God's provision of a substitute, one who bears the penalty of sin on behalf of the guilty.

1.2 The Origin of the Problem: The Fall

The need for atonement arises from the catastrophic events recorded in Genesis 3. When Adam and Eve disobeyed God, they introduced sin into the human condition. This act of rebellion resulted in spiritual death (separation from God), physical death (the eventual cessation of life), and a corruption of all creation.

- **Genesis 3:21** provides the first glimpse of atonement: "Unto Adam also and to his wife did the Lord God make coats of skins, and clothed them." This act involved the shedding of innocent blood to cover the nakedness and shame of Adam and Eve, foreshadowing the ultimate covering that would come through Christ.

1.3 God's Holiness and Human Sin

Scripture emphasizes God's absolute holiness: "Holy, holy, holy, is the Lord of hosts" (Isaiah 6:3). His perfection and righteousness demand that sin be punished. Habakkuk 1:13 declares, "Thou art of purer eyes than to behold evil, and canst not look on iniquity." Sin is not merely a breaking of God's law; it is an offense against His very nature.

- **Myer Pearlman**, in *Knowing the Doctrines of the Bible*, writes: "Sin is an affront to God's holiness and a violation of His righteous standard. Without the shedding of blood, there can be no remission, for sin requires a life to atone for its guilt."

1.4 The Consequences of Sin

1. **Separation from God**: Isaiah 59:2 says, "Your iniquities have separated between you and your

God." Sin creates an unbridgeable chasm between God and man.
2. **Guilt and Condemnation**: Romans 3:23 states, "For all have sinned, and come short of the glory of God." Humanity stands guilty and condemned before a holy God.
3. **Spiritual Death**: Romans 6:23 declares, "The wages of sin is death." Sin brings both physical and spiritual death.

1.5 The Theological Necessity of Atonement

The holiness of God requires that sin be punished, yet the love of God desires reconciliation with sinners. These two aspects of God's nature—justice and mercy—are perfectly harmonized in the atonement. As Myer Pearlman notes, "The cross is where the demands of divine justice and the pleas of divine mercy meet."

The apostle Paul captures this tension in Romans 3:26: "To declare, I say, at this time His righteousness: that He might be just, and the justifier of him which believeth in Jesus." God remains just by punishing sin, and He becomes the justifier by providing His Son as the atoning sacrifice.

1.6 A Preview of Redemption

Even in the midst of judgment, God revealed His plan for redemption. Genesis 3:15 contains the protoevangelium, the first promise of a Savior: "And I will put enmity between thee and the woman, and between thy seed and her seed; it shall bruise thy head, and thou shalt bruise his heel." This prophecy points to Christ, who would crush the power of sin and Satan through His atoning work.

Chapter 2: Old Testament Shadows of Atonement

2.1 The Old Testament Sacrificial System

The Old Testament sacrificial system provides a foundational understanding of atonement, offering a shadow of the ultimate work of Christ. Leviticus 16 details the Day of Atonement (Yom Kippur), a pivotal annual event in Israel's worship. On this day, the high priest entered the Holy of Holies to make atonement for the sins of the nation. This ceremony, ordained by God, was rich in symbolism and prophetic significance.

- **The Role of Sacrifices**: In Leviticus 17:11, God declares, "For the life of the flesh is in the blood: and I have given it to you upon the altar to make an atonement for your souls." The shedding of blood was essential because it symbolized the giving of life to atone for sin.
- **The High Priest as Mediator**: The high priest served as a mediator between God and the people, prefiguring Christ as the ultimate High Priest (Hebrews 9:11–12).

On the Day of Atonement, two central elements stood out:

1. **The Blood of the Sacrifice**: The blood of the bull and goat was sprinkled on the mercy seat to "cover" the sins of the people. This act symbolized the satisfaction of God's justice.
2. **The Scapegoat**: The high priest laid his hands on the head of the scapegoat, confessing the sins of the nation over it. The goat was then sent into the wilderness, symbolically carrying away the sins of the people (Leviticus 16:21–22).

2.2 Types and Shadows of Christ

The Old Testament sacrifices were never intended to be permanent solutions to sin. Hebrews 10:4 states, "For it is not possible that the blood of bulls and of goats should take away sins." Instead, they pointed forward to Christ, the perfect Lamb of God.

- **The Passover Lamb**: In Exodus 12, the blood of the Passover lamb protected the Israelites from the angel of death. This foreshadowed Jesus, "the Lamb of God, which taketh away the sin of the world" (John 1:29).
- **The Bronze Serpent**: Numbers 21 records how the Israelites were saved from death by looking at a bronze serpent lifted on a pole. This pointed to Christ being lifted on the cross, bringing salvation to all who believe (John 3:14–15).
- **The Binding of Isaac**: Genesis 22 portrays Abraham offering Isaac as a sacrifice, only for God to provide a ram as a substitute. This event

prefigured Christ as the substitute for humanity's sin.

2.3 The Blood Covenant

The concept of the blood covenant is central to understanding atonement. A covenant is a binding agreement between two parties, often sealed with blood. In the Old Testament, God established His covenant with Israel through the blood of sacrifices.

- **The Mosaic Covenant**: Exodus 24:8 records Moses sprinkling the blood of the covenant on the people, saying, "Behold the blood of the covenant, which the Lord hath made with you." This act foreshadowed the New Covenant, established through the blood of Christ (Luke 22:20).
- **Insights from *The Chemistry of the Blood***: M.R. DeHaan highlights the biological significance of blood as a carrier of life. This reinforces the spiritual truth that life is required to atone for sin.

2.4 Prophetic Foreshadowing of the Messiah

The Old Testament prophets foretold the coming of a Savior who would provide the ultimate atonement. Isaiah 53 is one of the most profound messianic prophecies, describing the Suffering Servant who would bear the sins of humanity.

- **Isaiah 53:5**: "But he was wounded for our transgressions, he was bruised for our iniquities: the chastisement of our peace was upon him; and with his stripes we are healed."
- **Psalm 22**: This psalm vividly describes the suffering of the Messiah, including details of His crucifixion, centuries before the event occurred.

2.5 Key Hebrew Terms for Atonement

A study of Hebrew words deepens our understanding of the Old Testament concept of atonement. Using *Strong's Concordance*, we find:

- **Kaphar** (H3722): "To cover, purge, make atonement." This term emphasizes the covering of sin through sacrifice.
- **Korban** (H7133): "Offering, gift." Sacrifices were seen as offerings brought near to God.
- **Chata'ah** (H2403): "Sin, sin offering." This word highlights both the act of sin and the provision for its cleansing.

2.6 God's Mercy in the Old Testament

While the sacrificial system emphasized the seriousness of sin, it also demonstrated God's mercy. The provision of sacrifices revealed God's desire to forgive and restore His people.

- **Psalm 103:10–12**: "He hath not dealt with us after our sins; nor rewarded us according to our

iniquities. For as the heaven is high above the earth, so great is his mercy toward them that fear him."
- **The Scarlet Thread of Redemption**: The recurring theme of bloodshed throughout the Old Testament reveals God's plan to redeem humanity through the ultimate sacrifice of Christ.

2.7 The Limitations of the Old Testament System

Despite its importance, the Old Testament system was inherently incomplete. It served as a temporary measure, pointing forward to the coming of Christ.

- **Hebrews 10:1**: "For the law having a shadow of good things to come, and not the very image of the things, can never with those sacrifices which they offered year by year continually make the comers thereunto perfect."
- **The Promise of a New Covenant**: Jeremiah 31:31–34 foretold a covenant where God would write His law on people's hearts and forgive their sins completely.

Chapter 3: God's Redemptive Nature

3.1 The Lamb Slain from the Foundation of the World

The atonement is not an afterthought in God's plan—it is central to His eternal purpose. Revelation 13:8 describes Jesus as "the Lamb slain from the foundation of the world." This phrase emphasizes that God's redemptive plan existed before the creation of the world, reflecting His omniscience and grace.

- **God's Eternal Purpose**: Ephesians 1:4–5 declares, "According as he hath chosen us in him before the foundation of the world… Having predestinated us unto the adoption of children by Jesus Christ to himself."
- **Divine Foreknowledge**: God knew humanity would fall into sin and prepared a way of salvation through the sacrifice of His Son.

3.2 God's Holiness and Justice

God's holiness is foundational to understanding the necessity of atonement. He is absolutely perfect, morally pure, and completely separate from sin. Isaiah 6:3 declares, "Holy, holy, holy, is the Lord of hosts: the whole earth is full of his glory." This holiness demands that sin be judged and punished.

- **The Nature of Divine Justice**: Deuteronomy 32:4 describes God as "a God of truth and without iniquity, just and right is He." Justice requires that sin be dealt with fairly, according to its seriousness.
- **The Wages of Sin**: Romans 6:23 states, "For the wages of sin is death." Sin's penalty is not only physical death but eternal separation from God.

3.3 God's Mercy and Love

While God is holy and just, He is also infinitely merciful and loving. His mercy does not negate His justice; rather, it works alongside it to provide a way of salvation.

- **The Balance of Mercy and Justice**: Psalm 85:10 beautifully expresses this harmony: "Mercy and truth are met together; righteousness and peace have kissed each other."
- **The Motivation of Love**: John 3:16 declares, "For God so loved the world, that He gave His only begotten Son, that whosoever believeth in Him should not perish, but have everlasting life." Love drove God to provide atonement for sinners.

3.4 Grace in the Old Testament

Although grace is often associated with the New Testament, it is present throughout the Old Testament as well. God's mercy and willingness to forgive are evident in His dealings with Israel and the provision of the sacrificial system.

- **The Ark of Noah**: Genesis 6:8 notes, "But Noah found grace in the eyes of the Lord." The ark served as a symbol of God's provision and salvation for those who trusted in Him.
- **The Passover Lamb**: God's grace spared the Israelites from the final plague in Egypt through the blood of the lamb (Exodus 12). This foreshadowed Christ's sacrificial death for humanity's sins.

3.5 Myer Pearlman's Insights on God's Nature

Myer Pearlman, in *Knowing the Doctrines of the Bible*, emphasizes that God's attributes of holiness, justice, love, and mercy are not in conflict but perfectly united in His redemptive work. Pearlman writes, "The cross is the ultimate demonstration of the harmony of God's attributes, where justice is satisfied, and love is revealed."

3.6 The Lamb Provided by God

The story of Abraham and Isaac in Genesis 22 illustrates God's redemptive nature. Abraham's willingness to sacrifice Isaac reflects the depth of his faith, but God intervenes, providing a ram as a substitute.

- **Genesis 22:14**: "And Abraham called the name of that place Jehovah-jireh: as it is said to this day, In the mount of the Lord it shall be seen."
- **Foreshadowing Christ**: Just as the ram was sacrificed in Isaac's place, Christ is the Lamb provided by God to take away the sin of the world.

3.7 God's Covenant of Redemption

God's redemptive nature is revealed in His covenants with humanity. These covenants demonstrate His commitment to redeem and restore what was lost through sin.

- **The Covenant with Abraham**: God's promise to bless all nations through Abraham's seed (Genesis 12:3) points to Christ as the ultimate fulfillment.
- **The New Covenant**: Jeremiah 31:31–34 foretells a covenant where God would write His law on hearts and forgive sins completely. This covenant was inaugurated by Christ's blood (Luke 22:20).

3.8 The Cost of Redemption

Atonement comes at a great cost, as it requires the shedding of blood and the giving of life. Hebrews 9:22 states, "Without shedding of blood is no remission."

God's willingness to pay this price reveals the depth of His love and commitment to redeem humanity.

- **Christ's Sacrifice**: 1 Peter 1:18–19 declares, "Forasmuch as ye know that ye were not redeemed with corruptible things, as silver and gold…but with the precious blood of Christ, as of a lamb without blemish and without spot."
- **Insights from *The Chemistry of the Blood***: M.R. DeHaan emphasizes the unique nature of Christ's blood, which was both human and divine. This blood was not tainted by sin, making it the perfect offering for atonement.

3.9 Redemption and Worship

The proper response to God's redemptive work is worship. Revelation 5:9 records the song of the redeemed: "Thou art worthy…for thou wast slain, and hast redeemed us to God by thy blood out of every kindred, and tongue, and people, and nation."

Chapter 4: Jesus as the Perfect Sacrifice

4.1 The Incarnation and Sinlessness of Christ

For the atonement to be effective, the Savior must be both fully God and fully man. Only a perfect, sinless sacrifice could satisfy the demands of God's justice and provide salvation for sinful humanity. Jesus Christ, as the incarnate Son of God, is the perfect embodiment of both divinity and humanity.

- **The Necessity of the Incarnation**: Hebrews 2:14 states, "Forasmuch then as the children are partakers of flesh and blood, he also himself likewise took part of the same." Christ's full humanity was essential to identify with the human condition and serve as the perfect representative for humanity before God.
- **Sinlessness**: Hebrews 4:15 emphasizes that Christ "was in all points tempted like as we are, yet without sin." Jesus' sinlessness was crucial because only a pure, unblemished sacrifice could bear the weight of sin for others.

The doctrine of the hypostatic union, the belief that Christ is both fully God and fully man, is foundational to understanding the atonement. As Myer Pearlman writes in *Knowing the Doctrines of the Bible*, "The sinless humanity of Christ made Him the ideal sacrifice, and His divine nature ensured the adequacy of the sacrifice to meet the eternal demands of a holy God."

4.2 John the Baptist's Declaration: "Behold the Lamb of God"

The mission of Jesus was made clear from the very beginning of His earthly ministry. In John 1:29, John the Baptist, seeing Jesus, proclaimed, "Behold the Lamb of God, which taketh away the sin of the world." This statement identifies Jesus as the fulfillment of the sacrificial system established in the Old Testament.

- **The Lamb of God**: Jesus is the ultimate fulfillment of the Passover lamb, whose blood was shed to protect the Israelites from death (Exodus 12). In the same way, Jesus' sacrificial death protects believers from eternal death and provides a way for reconciliation with God.
- **The Scope of His Sacrifice**: John emphasizes that Jesus came to "take away the sin of the world." His sacrifice was not limited to a specific group of people but was offered to all who would believe.

4.3 Christ as High Priest and Sacrifice

The Book of Hebrews presents Christ as both the High Priest and the sacrifice. As High Priest, Jesus intercedes for humanity, offering Himself as the perfect and final sacrifice for sin.

- **The Role of the High Priest**: In the Old Testament, the high priest was the mediator between God and the people. He would enter the Holy of Holies once a year, offering the blood of sacrifices to atone for the sins of the nation. Hebrews 9:11–12 contrasts Christ's work with the Old Testament priesthood: "But Christ being come an high priest…by His own blood He entered in once into the holy place, having obtained eternal redemption for us."
- **The Perfect Sacrifice**: The high priests of old had to offer sacrifices repeatedly, but Jesus, as both priest and sacrifice, made a once-for-all offering that secured eternal redemption. Hebrews 10:12 states, "But this man, after he had offered one sacrifice for sins forever, sat down on the right hand of God."

4.4 The Significance of Christ's Blood

The blood of Jesus is the central element of His atoning work. Blood, throughout Scripture, symbolizes life and is necessary for atonement (Leviticus 17:11). The blood of Christ not only covers sin but also cleanses and redeems.

- **The Life is in the Blood**: Leviticus 17:11 reveals that "the life of the flesh is in the blood," and this truth points to the essential role of Jesus' blood in the atonement. His blood was shed to give life to those who were dead in trespasses and sins (Ephesians 2:1).

- **The Power of Christ's Blood**: 1 John 1:7 declares, "The blood of Jesus Christ his Son cleanseth us from all sin." The cleansing power of His blood removes the guilt and stain of sin, reconciling believers to God.
- **M.R. DeHaan's *The Chemistry of the Blood***: In *The Chemistry of the Blood*, DeHaan emphasizes the uniqueness of Christ's blood. Unlike the blood of ordinary humans, which is tainted by sin, Christ's blood was sinless. DeHaan writes, "The purity of His blood made it the only blood that could cleanse humanity from its sin."

4.5 The Cross: The Crux of Atonement

The cross stands as the central event in human history, where Jesus, the perfect sacrifice, gave His life to atone for sin. The cross is the ultimate expression of God's love, justice, and mercy.

- **The Suffering of Christ**: Isaiah 53:5 states, "He was wounded for our transgressions, he was bruised for our iniquities: the chastisement of our peace was upon him; and with his stripes we are healed." On the cross, Jesus bore the physical, emotional, and spiritual suffering of humanity's sin.
- **The Substitutionary Atonement**: 2 Corinthians 5:21 explains, "For he hath made him to be sin for us, who knew no sin; that we might be made the righteousness of God in him." Jesus became

our substitute, taking the punishment we deserved, so that we could receive the righteousness of God.

4.6 The Cross and the Glory of God

While the cross is a symbol of suffering, it is also a symbol of glory. Through the cross, God's justice is satisfied, His holiness is vindicated, and His love is revealed. Jesus' death on the cross was not a tragic accident; it was the fulfillment of God's eternal plan for redemption.

- **John 12:23–24**: Jesus speaks of His death as a glorification: "The hour is come, that the Son of man should be glorified. Verily, verily, I say unto you, Except a corn of wheat fall into the ground and die, it abideth alone: but if it die, it bringeth forth much fruit."
- **The Triumph of the Cross**: Colossians 2:14–15 reveals the cosmic victory achieved through the cross: "Blotting out the handwriting of ordinances that was against us, which was contrary to us, and took it out of the way, nailing it to his cross; And having spoiled principalities and powers, he made a shew of them openly, triumphing over them in it."

4.7 The Resurrection and Atonement

The resurrection of Jesus confirms the effectiveness of His atoning work. Romans 4:25 says, "Who was delivered for our offenses, and was raised again for our justification." Christ's resurrection proves that sin has been defeated and that believers are justified before God.

- **The Victory of Resurrection**: The resurrection is not just a demonstration of Christ's power over death, but a declaration that the price for sin has been fully paid and accepted by God.

Chapter 5: The Power of the Blood

5.1 The Centrality of Blood in Scripture

The Bible consistently emphasizes the significance of blood in God's plan for redemption. From the Old Testament sacrificial system to the New Testament fulfillment in Christ, blood is central to atonement, purification, and reconciliation.

- **Leviticus 17:11**: "For the life of the flesh is in the blood: and I have given it to you upon the altar to make an atonement for your souls: for it is the blood that maketh an atonement for the soul."
- **Hebrews 9:22**: "And almost all things are by the law purged with blood; and without shedding of blood is no remission."

The shedding of blood is not merely symbolic; it reflects the divine principle that sin incurs a penalty—death—and that life must be given to atone for sin.

5.2 Insights from Science and Theology

In *The Chemistry of the Blood*, M.R. DeHaan draws fascinating parallels between the biological properties of blood and its theological significance.

- **Blood as Life**: DeHaan explains that blood is essential for sustaining life, carrying oxygen and nutrients to every part of the body. Similarly, the blood of Christ sustains spiritual life, bringing forgiveness, cleansing, and restoration to the soul.
- **Purifying Power**: Just as physical blood removes waste and toxins from the body, Christ's blood purifies believers from the guilt and stain of sin. 1 John 1:7 declares, "The blood of Jesus Christ his Son cleanseth us from all sin."
- **The Uniqueness of Christ's Blood**: DeHaan emphasizes that Jesus' blood was untainted by sin, making it uniquely powerful. As the Son of God, His blood was divine and sufficient to atone for the sins of the world.

5.3 The Blood in the Old Testament

The Old Testament sacrificial system was built on the principle of substitutionary atonement, where the blood of an animal was shed in place of the sinner. These sacrifices were temporary and pointed forward to the ultimate sacrifice of Christ.

- **The Passover Lamb**: Exodus 12 recounts the institution of the Passover, where the blood of a lamb was applied to the doorposts, sparing the Israelites from the plague of death. This act foreshadowed Jesus as the Lamb of God, whose blood delivers believers from eternal death.

- **The Day of Atonement**: On Yom Kippur, the high priest would sprinkle the blood of a sacrifice on the mercy seat to atone for the sins of the people (Leviticus 16). This ritual symbolized the covering of sin and pointed to Christ's ultimate atonement.

5.4 The Blood of Christ in the New Testament

In the New Testament, the blood of Christ takes center stage as the means of redemption, justification, and reconciliation.

- **Redemption**: Ephesians 1:7 declares, "In whom we have redemption through his blood, the forgiveness of sins, according to the riches of his grace." Through His blood, Jesus paid the price to free humanity from the bondage of sin.
- **Justification**: Romans 5:9 states, "Much more then, being now justified by his blood, we shall be saved from wrath through him." The blood of Christ removes the guilt of sin, allowing believers to stand righteous before God.
- **Reconciliation**: Colossians 1:20 teaches, "And, having made peace through the blood of his cross, by him to reconcile all things unto himself." Through the blood of Christ, the broken relationship between God and humanity is restored.

5.5 The Purifying Power of the Blood

The blood of Christ not only justifies but also sanctifies and cleanses believers, enabling them to live holy lives.

- **Cleansing from Sin**: 1 John 1:7 affirms, "The blood of Jesus Christ his Son cleanseth us from all sin." This cleansing is both positional (justification) and ongoing (sanctification).
- **Access to God**: Hebrews 10:19 declares, "Having therefore, brethren, boldness to enter into the holiest by the blood of Jesus." The blood of Christ grants believers direct access to God, tearing down the barriers of sin.

5.6 The Blood and Covenant

The blood of Christ inaugurates the New Covenant, fulfilling the promises of the Old Testament and establishing an eternal relationship between God and His people.

- **The Institution of the New Covenant**: During the Last Supper, Jesus declared, "This is my blood of the new testament, which is shed for many for the remission of sins" (Matthew 26:28). His blood sealed the covenant, offering forgiveness and eternal life to all who believe.
- **The Eternal Covenant**: Hebrews 13:20 refers to the "blood of the everlasting covenant," emphasizing the permanence and sufficiency of Christ's atonement.

5.7 The Blood and Victory

The blood of Christ is not only the means of salvation but also the source of victory over sin, Satan, and death.

- **Victory Over Sin**: Romans 6:10 declares, "For in that he died, he died unto sin once: but in that he liveth, he liveth unto God." The blood of Christ breaks the power of sin, enabling believers to live in freedom.
- **Victory Over Satan**: Revelation 12:11 proclaims, "And they overcame him by the blood of the Lamb, and by the word of their testimony." The blood of Christ is a weapon against the enemy, securing victory for believers.
- **Victory Over Death**: Through His resurrection, Christ demonstrated the ultimate power of His blood to conquer death. 1 Corinthians 15:55–57 celebrates this victory: "O death, where is thy sting? O grave, where is thy victory?… Thanks be to God, which giveth us the victory through our Lord Jesus Christ."

5.8 Worship Through the Blood

The proper response to the power of Christ's blood is worship and gratitude. Revelation 5:9 records the song of the redeemed: "Thou art worthy…for thou wast slain, and hast redeemed us to God by thy blood."

- **The Eternal Song**: The blood of Christ will remain the central theme of worship in eternity, as the redeemed glorify the Lamb who was slain.

Chapter 6: The Cross: The Crux of Atonement

6.1 The Centrality of the Cross

The cross is the pivotal event in human history and the crux of the atonement. It is the place where God's holiness, justice, love, and mercy converge. Without the cross, there is no forgiveness, no reconciliation, and no hope. Paul declared, "But God forbid that I should glory, save in the cross of our Lord Jesus Christ" (Galatians 6:14). The cross is not merely a symbol of suffering but a demonstration of God's redemptive power.

6.2 The Suffering of Christ

The physical, emotional, and spiritual suffering Jesus endured on the cross underscores the weight of sin and the cost of redemption.

- **Physical Suffering**: The crucifixion was a brutal method of execution designed to maximize pain and humiliation. Isaiah 52:14 prophesied, "His visage was so marred more than any man, and his form more than the sons of men."
- **Emotional Suffering**: Jesus was mocked, abandoned, and betrayed by those closest to Him. He experienced profound loneliness, crying out,

"My God, my God, why hast thou forsaken me?" (Matthew 27:46).
- **Spiritual Suffering**: On the cross, Jesus bore the full weight of humanity's sin. 2 Corinthians 5:21 states, "For he hath made him to be sin for us, who knew no sin; that we might be made the righteousness of God in him."

6.3 The Substitutionary Atonement

At the heart of the cross is the doctrine of substitutionary atonement, which teaches that Christ took the place of sinners, bearing the punishment they deserved.

- **Isaiah 53:5**: "But he was wounded for our transgressions, he was bruised for our iniquities: the chastisement of our peace was upon him; and with his stripes we are healed."
- **1 Peter 2:24**: "Who his own self bare our sins in his own body on the tree, that we, being dead to sins, should live unto righteousness: by whose stripes ye were healed."
- **Romans 3:25**: "Whom God hath set forth to be a propitiation through faith in his blood." The term "propitiation" means a sacrifice that turns away wrath, emphasizing that Christ satisfied the demands of God's justice.

6.4 The Cross and the Justice of God

The cross demonstrates that God's justice cannot be compromised. Sin must be punished, and the penalty is death. However, in His mercy, God provided a substitute.

- **Romans 6:23**: "For the wages of sin is death; but the gift of God is eternal life through Jesus Christ our Lord."
- **Romans 3:26**: "To declare, I say, at this time his righteousness: that he might be just, and the justifier of him which believeth in Jesus." God remains just by punishing sin and merciful by justifying those who place their faith in Christ.

6.5 The Cross and the Love of God

The cross is the ultimate expression of God's love for humanity. Romans 5:8 declares, "But God commendeth his love toward us, in that, while we were yet sinners, Christ died for us."

- **John 3:16**: "For God so loved the world, that he gave his only begotten Son, that whosoever believeth in him should not perish, but have everlasting life."
- **1 John 4:10**: "Herein is love, not that we loved God, but that he loved us, and sent his Son to be the propitiation for our sins."

God's love is not sentimental but sacrificial, demonstrated through the suffering and death of His Son.

6.6 The Victory of the Cross

While the cross was a place of suffering, it was also the site of victory. Through His death, Jesus triumphed over sin, death, and Satan.

- **Victory Over Sin**: Colossians 2:14 declares that Christ "blotted out the handwriting of ordinances that was against us, which was contrary to us, and took it out of the way, nailing it to his cross."
- **Victory Over Death**: Hebrews 2:14–15 reveals that through His death, Christ destroyed "him that had the power of death, that is, the devil," and delivered those who were in bondage to the fear of death.
- **Victory Over Satan**: Colossians 2:15 proclaims, "And having spoiled principalities and powers, he made a shew of them openly, triumphing over them in it."

6.7 Christ's Cry: "It Is Finished"

One of the most profound statements Jesus made on the cross was, "It is finished" (John 19:30). This declaration signifies the completion of His redemptive work.

- **Fulfillment of Prophecy**: Christ's death fulfilled the messianic prophecies of the Old Testament, such as Isaiah 53 and Psalm 22.
- **Completion of Redemption**: The phrase "It is finished" (Greek: *tetelestai*) was often used in

financial transactions to mean "paid in full." Jesus' death fully satisfied the debt of sin.
- **The End of the Sacrificial System**: The tearing of the temple veil at Christ's death (Matthew 27:51) symbolized the end of the Old Testament sacrificial system and the opening of direct access to God through Christ.

6.8 The Cross and the Believer

The cross not only secures salvation but also shapes the life of the believer. It calls for a life of gratitude, humility, and self-sacrifice.

- **A Call to Discipleship**: Jesus said, "If any man will come after me, let him deny himself, and take up his cross daily, and follow me" (Luke 9:23). The cross is not only an instrument of salvation but also a model for Christian living.
- **Living in Light of the Cross**: Galatians 2:20 emphasizes the believer's union with Christ: "I am crucified with Christ: nevertheless I live; yet not I, but Christ liveth in me."
- **Proclaiming the Cross**: Paul declared, "For I determined not to know any thing among you, save Jesus Christ, and him crucified" (1 Corinthians 2:2). The cross is central to the believer's message and mission.

6.9 The Cross and Eternal Worship

The significance of the cross extends into eternity. Revelation 5:9–10 records the song of the redeemed: "Thou art worthy to take the book, and to open the seals thereof: for thou wast slain, and hast redeemed us to God by thy blood."

- **Eternal Glory of the Lamb**: Christ's sacrificial death will remain the focal point of worship in heaven, as the redeemed praise Him for His atoning work.
- **The Cross and God's Ultimate Plan**: The cross is not an end in itself but part of God's larger plan to reconcile all things to Himself (Colossians 1:20).

Chapter 7: The Resurrection and Atonement

7.1 The Resurrection: A Vindication of the Cross

The resurrection of Jesus Christ is inseparable from the atonement. While the cross secured salvation, the resurrection validated and demonstrated its power. Without the resurrection, the cross would have been a tragedy, but with it, the cross becomes a triumph.

- **Romans 4:25**: "Who was delivered for our offences, and was raised again for our justification." The resurrection proves that Jesus' sacrifice was sufficient and accepted by God.
- **1 Corinthians 15:17**: "And if Christ be not raised, your faith is vain; ye are yet in your sins." Paul emphasizes that the resurrection is essential for the efficacy of the atonement.

The resurrection vindicates Jesus as the Son of God and confirms the truth of His claims. Romans 1:4 declares that Jesus was "declared to be the Son of God with power…by the resurrection from the dead."

7.2 The Power of the Resurrection

The resurrection demonstrates God's power over sin, death, and Satan. It is the cornerstone of Christian hope and the guarantee of eternal life for believers.

- **Victory Over Sin**: The resurrection proves that Jesus conquered sin. 1 Corinthians 15:55–57 declares, "O death, where is thy sting? O grave, where is thy victory?... Thanks be to God, which giveth us the victory through our Lord Jesus Christ."
- **Victory Over Death**: Christ's resurrection ensures the believer's resurrection. John 11:25–26 records Jesus' words: "I am the resurrection, and the life: he that believeth in me, though he were dead, yet shall he live."
- **Victory Over Satan**: Through the resurrection, Jesus defeated Satan's power. Hebrews 2:14 states, "That through death he might destroy him that had the power of death, that is, the devil."

7.3 The Resurrection and Justification

The resurrection is directly tied to the believer's justification. It is the divine declaration that the debt of sin has been paid in full.

- **Legal Declaration**: Justification means being declared righteous before God. The resurrection is the evidence that Christ's atoning sacrifice was accepted by God, satisfying His justice.

- **Romans 8:33–34**: "Who shall lay any thing to the charge of God's elect? It is God that justifieth. Who is he that condemneth? It is Christ that died, yea rather, that is risen again, who is even at the right hand of God, who also maketh intercession for us."

7.4 The Living Intercessor

Christ's resurrection establishes Him as the living High Priest who intercedes for believers. Unlike the Old Testament priests who were subject to death, Jesus lives forever to mediate on behalf of His people.

- **Hebrews 7:25**: "Wherefore he is able also to save them to the uttermost that come unto God by him, seeing he ever liveth to make intercession for them."
- **The Ascended Lord**: After His resurrection, Jesus ascended to the right hand of God, where He continues His priestly ministry (Romans 8:34; Acts 1:9–11).

7.5 The Firstfruits of the Resurrection

Jesus' resurrection is described as the "firstfruits" of those who have died, signifying that His resurrection is the guarantee of the believer's future resurrection.

- **1 Corinthians 15:20**: "But now is Christ risen from the dead, and become the firstfruits of them that slept."

- **The Hope of Glory**: Colossians 1:27 speaks of "Christ in you, the hope of glory," emphasizing the believer's hope of eternal life and resurrection.

7.6 The Resurrection and the New Covenant

The resurrection is central to the fulfillment of the New Covenant, inaugurated through Christ's blood and sealed by His victory over death.

- **A New Relationship with God**: The resurrection brings believers into a living relationship with God. Romans 6:4 says, "Therefore we are buried with him by baptism into death: that like as Christ was raised up from the dead by the glory of the Father, even so we also should walk in newness of life."
- **The Spirit's Role**: The resurrection paved the way for the coming of the Holy Spirit, who empowers believers to live in the light of the New Covenant (John 14:16–17; Acts 2:32–33).

7.7 Living in Resurrection Power

The resurrection not only secures the believer's future but also transforms their present life. Through union with Christ, believers share in His resurrection power.

- **Romans 6:5**: "For if we have been planted together in the likeness of his death, we shall be also in the likeness of his resurrection."

- **Ephesians 1:19–20**: Paul prays that believers may know "the exceeding greatness of his power to us-ward who believe, according to the working of his mighty power, which he wrought in Christ, when he raised him from the dead."

The resurrection empowers believers to live victoriously over sin and to fulfill God's purpose for their lives.

7.8 The Resurrection and Eternal Life

The resurrection guarantees eternal life for all who believe in Christ. It is the foundation of Christian hope and the assurance of a future with God.

- **John 14:19**: Jesus said, "Because I live, ye shall live also."
- **1 Thessalonians 4:14**: "For if we believe that Jesus died and rose again, even so them also which sleep in Jesus will God bring with him."

The resurrection transforms death from a curse into a gateway to eternal life.

7.9 Worship in Light of the Resurrection

The resurrection is not only a theological truth but also a cause for worship and celebration. It is the reason for the church's existence and the focus of its proclamation.

- **The Apostolic Message**: The apostles consistently preached the resurrection of Christ

as the cornerstone of the gospel (Acts 2:32; 4:33).
- **Revelation 1:18**: Jesus declares, "I am he that liveth, and was dead; and, behold, I am alive for evermore, Amen; and have the keys of hell and of death."

The resurrection inspires believers to worship Christ as the risen Lord and to proclaim His victory to the world.

Chapter 8: Atonement and Justification

8.1 Understanding Justification

Justification is a legal term that signifies being declared righteous in the eyes of God. It is not based on human merit or works but on the finished work of Jesus Christ on the cross. The atonement is the basis of justification, and faith is the means by which it is received.

- **Romans 3:23–24**: "For all have sinned, and come short of the glory of God; being justified freely by his grace through the redemption that is in Christ Jesus."
- **Definition**: Justification is God's act of pardoning sinners and imputing the righteousness of Christ to them through faith.

Myer Pearlman, in *Knowing the Doctrines of the Bible*, writes, "Justification is not the making of a person righteous in themselves, but the declaration that they are righteous before God because of the work of Christ on their behalf."

8.2 The Legal Nature of Justification

The concept of justification originates in the courtroom, where a judge declares a defendant "not guilty." In the spiritual sense, God, the ultimate Judge, declares sinners righteous because the penalty for their sins has been paid by Christ.

- **Romans 8:33–34**: "Who shall lay any thing to the charge of God's elect? It is God that justifieth. Who is he that condemneth? It is Christ that died, yea rather, that is risen again."
- **Imputed Righteousness**: Through justification, the righteousness of Christ is credited to the believer's account. 2 Corinthians 5:21 explains, "For he hath made him to be sin for us, who knew no sin; that we might be made the righteousness of God in him."

8.3 The Role of Faith in Justification

Faith is the means by which justification is received. It is not a work that earns justification but the hand that receives the gift of God's grace.

- **Romans 5:1**: "Therefore being justified by faith, we have peace with God through our Lord Jesus Christ."
- **Faith Defined**: Faith involves trusting in the person and work of Christ for salvation. Ephesians 2:8–9 affirms, "For by grace are ye saved through faith; and that not of yourselves: it is the gift of God: not of works, lest any man should boast."

Faith does not add to Christ's work but rests entirely upon it. Justification is by faith alone, apart from works, as Paul emphasizes in Galatians 2:16: "A man is not justified by the works of the law, but by the faith of Jesus Christ."

8.4 Grace and Justification

Justification is an act of God's grace, meaning it is undeserved and freely given. It is based entirely on His initiative and not on human effort.

- **Romans 3:24**: "Being justified freely by his grace through the redemption that is in Christ Jesus."
- **The Gift of Grace**: Grace is God's unmerited favor toward sinners. As Titus 3:5–7 explains, "Not by works of righteousness which we have done, but according to his mercy he saved us…that being justified by his grace, we should be made heirs according to the hope of eternal life."

8.5 Justification Through the Blood of Christ

The atonement provides the basis for justification. Without the shedding of blood, there could be no forgiveness or justification.

- **Romans 5:9**: "Much more then, being now justified by his blood, we shall be saved from wrath through him."

- **The Role of the Cross**: At the cross, Jesus bore the penalty of sin, satisfying the demands of God's justice. As a result, God can justify sinners while remaining just. Romans 3:26 declares, "That he might be just, and the justifier of him which believeth in Jesus."

8.6 The Results of Justification

Justification brings about profound spiritual and practical benefits for the believer. These include:

1. **Peace with God**: Romans 5:1 assures, "Therefore being justified by faith, we have peace with God through our Lord Jesus Christ." The hostility caused by sin is replaced with reconciliation.
2. **Freedom from Condemnation**: Romans 8:1 proclaims, "There is therefore now no condemnation to them which are in Christ Jesus."
3. **Access to God**: Through justification, believers have direct access to God's presence. Ephesians 2:18 states, "For through him we both have access by one Spirit unto the Father."
4. **The Hope of Glory**: Justification guarantees eternal life and glorification. Romans 8:30 declares, "Whom he justified, them he also glorified."

8.7 Justification and Works

While justification is by faith alone, true faith produces good works as its evidence and fruit. Good works are not the basis of justification but the result of it.

- **James 2:17**: "Even so faith, if it hath not works, is dead, being alone."
- **Ephesians 2:10**: "For we are his workmanship, created in Christ Jesus unto good works, which God hath before ordained that we should walk in them."

As Martin Luther explained, "We are saved by faith alone, but the faith that saves is never alone."

8.8 Justification and Sanctification

Justification and sanctification are distinct yet inseparable aspects of salvation. Justification is a one-time legal declaration of righteousness, while sanctification is the ongoing process of being made holy.

- **1 Corinthians 6:11**: "But ye are washed, but ye are sanctified, but ye are justified in the name of the Lord Jesus, and by the Spirit of our God."
- **Living Out Justification**: Sanctification is the practical outworking of justification, as believers grow in holiness and conformity to Christ.

8.9 The Glory of God in Justification

The ultimate purpose of justification is to bring glory to God. By justifying sinners, God reveals His holiness, justice, love, and mercy in a way that magnifies His character.

- **Romans 11:36**: "For of him, and through him, and to him, are all things: to whom be glory for ever. Amen."
- **Revelation 5:9**: In eternity, the redeemed will worship Christ, saying, "Thou art worthy…for thou wast slain, and hast redeemed us to God by thy blood."

Chapter 9: Sanctification and the Atonement

9.1 Understanding Sanctification

Sanctification is the process by which believers are set apart for God and transformed into the likeness of Christ. While justification addresses the believer's legal standing before God, sanctification focuses on their moral and spiritual transformation.

- **Definition**: Sanctification means "to make holy" or "to set apart." The Greek word *hagiasmos* (Strong's G38) signifies both a position (being set apart for God) and a process (becoming more like Christ).
- **1 Thessalonians 4:3**: "For this is the will of God, even your sanctification, that ye should abstain from fornication."

Sanctification flows directly from the atonement, as the blood of Christ not only justifies but also purifies believers, enabling them to live holy lives.

9.2 The Twofold Nature of Sanctification

Sanctification has both a positional and a progressive aspect, each rooted in the atoning work of Christ.

1. **Positional Sanctification**: At the moment of salvation, believers are declared holy and set apart for God.
   - **Hebrews 10:10**: "By the which will we are sanctified through the offering of the body of Jesus Christ once for all."
   - This is a completed act, accomplished through the blood of Christ and applied by faith.
2. **Progressive Sanctification**: Over time, believers grow in holiness and conformity to Christ.
   - **2 Corinthians 3:18**: "But we all…are changed into the same image from glory to glory, even as by the Spirit of the Lord."
   - This is an ongoing work of the Holy Spirit, requiring the believer's cooperation.

9.3 The Role of the Blood of Christ in Sanctification

The atonement provides the foundation for sanctification. The blood of Christ not only cleanses believers from sin but also empowers them to live holy lives.

- **Cleansing from Sin**: 1 John 1:7 declares, "The blood of Jesus Christ his Son cleanseth us from all sin." This cleansing is both positional and continual.
- **Empowerment for Holiness**: Hebrews 9:14 explains that the blood of Christ purges the

conscience from dead works, enabling believers to serve the living God.

M.R. DeHaan, in *The Chemistry of the Blood*, highlights how the purifying power of blood in the human body mirrors the spiritual cleansing provided by Christ's blood. Just as physical blood removes toxins, Christ's blood removes the guilt and defilement of sin.

9.4 The Work of the Holy Spirit in Sanctification

Sanctification is primarily the work of the Holy Spirit, who applies the benefits of the atonement to the believer's life.

- **Indwelling of the Spirit**: At salvation, the Holy Spirit takes up residence in the believer, enabling them to live a life pleasing to God (1 Corinthians 6:19–20).
- **Transforming Power**: The Spirit works to conform believers to the image of Christ. Galatians 5:22–23 lists the fruit of the Spirit as evidence of this transformation.
- **Ephesians 5:26**: The Word of God, empowered by the Spirit, cleanses and sanctifies believers: "That he might sanctify and cleanse it with the washing of water by the word."

9.5 The Believer's Role in Sanctification

While sanctification is ultimately God's work, believers are called to participate actively in the process.

- **Surrender to God**: Romans 12:1 urges believers to present their bodies as living sacrifices, holy and acceptable to God.
- **Obedience to God's Word**: Psalm 119:11 states, "Thy word have I hid in mine heart, that I might not sin against thee." Scripture is a vital tool in the sanctification process.
- **Walking in the Spirit**: Galatians 5:16 commands, "Walk in the Spirit, and ye shall not fulfill the lust of the flesh." Dependence on the Holy Spirit is essential for victory over sin.

9.6 Victory Over Sin Through the Atonement

The atonement breaks the power of sin, enabling believers to live in freedom and victory.

- **Romans 6:6–7**: "Knowing this, that our old man is crucified with him, that the body of sin might be destroyed, that henceforth we should not serve sin. For he that is dead is freed from sin."
- **Union with Christ**: Through the atonement, believers are united with Christ in His death and resurrection. This union empowers them to live new lives. Romans 6:4 states, "Therefore we are buried with him by baptism into death: that like as Christ was raised up from the dead…even so we also should walk in newness of life."

9.7 The Goal of Sanctification: Christlikeness

The ultimate aim of sanctification is to conform believers to the image of Christ, reflecting His character and glory.

- **Romans 8:29**: "For whom he did foreknow, he also did predestinate to be conformed to the image of his Son."
- **2 Peter 1:3–4**: God has given believers everything they need to live godly lives, enabling them to "be partakers of the divine nature."

9.8 Sanctification and Community

Sanctification is not merely an individual process; it takes place within the context of the Christian community.

- **Mutual Edification**: Believers are called to encourage and build one another up in their walk with Christ (Hebrews 10:24–25).
- **Unity in Holiness**: Ephesians 4:13 emphasizes the goal of unity in the faith and knowledge of Christ, leading to maturity.

9.9 The Completion of Sanctification

Sanctification will be completed when believers are glorified and fully conformed to the image of Christ.

- **1 Thessalonians 5:23–24**: "And the very God of peace sanctify you wholly; and I pray God your whole spirit and soul and body be preserved blameless unto the coming of our Lord Jesus Christ. Faithful is he that calleth you, who also will do it."
- **1 John 3:2**: "Beloved, now are we the sons of God, and it doth not yet appear what we shall be: but we know that, when he shall appear, we shall be like him; for we shall see him as he is."

Chapter 10: The Atonement and Reconciliation

10.1 Understanding Reconciliation

Reconciliation is the restoration of a broken relationship. In the biblical context, it refers to the mending of the relationship between God and humanity, which was fractured by sin. The atonement of Christ makes reconciliation possible by removing the barrier of sin and enabling humanity to have peace with God.

- **2 Corinthians 5:18–19**: "And all things are of God, who hath reconciled us to himself by Jesus Christ, and hath given to us the ministry of reconciliation; to wit, that God was in Christ, reconciling the world unto himself, not imputing their trespasses unto them."
- **Definition**: The Greek word for reconciliation, *katallagé* (Strong's G2643), means "restoration to favor" or "exchange." Through Christ, the hostility between God and humanity is exchanged for peace and fellowship.

10.2 The Necessity of Reconciliation

The need for reconciliation arises from the alienation caused by sin. Sin not only separates humanity from God but also creates enmity between God and sinners.

- **Isaiah 59:2**: "But your iniquities have separated between you and your God, and your sins have hid his face from you, that he will not hear."
- **Colossians 1:21**: "And you, that were sometime alienated and enemies in your mind by wicked works, yet now hath he reconciled."
- **God's Holiness**: Because God is holy and just, He cannot overlook sin. Reconciliation required a solution that upheld His justice while extending His mercy.

10.3 The Means of Reconciliation

Reconciliation is made possible through the atoning work of Christ, who bore the penalty of sin on the cross.

- **Romans 5:10**: "For if, when we were enemies, we were reconciled to God by the death of his Son, much more, being reconciled, we shall be saved by his life."
- **The Role of the Cross**: On the cross, Jesus removed the barrier of sin, satisfying God's justice and making reconciliation possible. Colossians 1:20 declares, "And, having made peace through the blood of his cross, by him to reconcile all things unto himself."

- **The Substitutionary Sacrifice**: Christ became the mediator between God and humanity by taking humanity's sin upon Himself. 1 Timothy 2:5 says, "For there is one God, and one mediator between God and men, the man Christ Jesus."

10.4 Reconciliation and Peace with God

One of the primary results of reconciliation is peace with God. The enmity caused by sin is replaced with a harmonious relationship.

- **Romans 5:1**: "Therefore being justified by faith, we have peace with God through our Lord Jesus Christ."
- **Ephesians 2:14–16**: "For he is our peace, who hath made both one, and hath broken down the middle wall of partition between us…that he might reconcile both unto God in one body by the cross."

This peace is not merely the absence of conflict but the presence of a restored relationship characterized by love, trust, and communion with God.

10.5 Reconciliation and Horizontal Relationships

The atonement not only reconciles believers to God but also transforms their relationships with one another. Reconciliation with God becomes the basis for reconciliation among people.

- **Matthew 5:23–24**: Jesus teaches the importance of seeking reconciliation with others: "Therefore if thou bring thy gift to the altar, and there rememberest that thy brother hath ought against thee; leave there thy gift before the altar, and go thy way; first be reconciled to thy brother."
- **Ephesians 4:32**: "And be ye kind one to another, tenderhearted, forgiving one another, even as God for Christ's sake hath forgiven you."

The atonement compels believers to forgive and seek peace with others, reflecting the reconciliation they have received from God.

10.6 The Universal Scope of Reconciliation

Reconciliation through Christ extends beyond individuals to all of creation. Sin affected not only humanity but also the created order, and Christ's work of reconciliation will ultimately restore all things.

- **Romans 8:21**: "Because the creature itself also shall be delivered from the bondage of corruption into the glorious liberty of the children of God."
- **Colossians 1:20**: "And, having made peace through the blood of his cross, by him to reconcile all things unto himself."

This cosmic reconciliation will be fully realized when Christ returns and establishes His eternal kingdom, bringing harmony and peace to the entire universe.

10.7 The Ministry of Reconciliation

Believers are called to participate in God's work of reconciliation by proclaiming the gospel and living as ambassadors of Christ.

- **2 Corinthians 5:18–20**: "And hath given to us the ministry of reconciliation…Now then we are ambassadors for Christ, as though God did beseech you by us: we pray you in Christ's stead, be ye reconciled to God."
- **The Gospel of Peace**: Ephesians 6:15 describes the gospel as "the preparation of the gospel of peace." Sharing the message of reconciliation is a vital aspect of the believer's mission.

10.8 The Cost of Reconciliation

Reconciliation came at a great cost—the death of God's Son. This underscores the seriousness of sin and the depth of God's love.

- **1 Peter 3:18**: "For Christ also hath once suffered for sins, the just for the unjust, that he might bring us to God."
- **John 15:13**: "Greater love hath no man than this, that a man lay down his life for his friends."

The cost of reconciliation highlights the value God places on restoring His relationship with humanity.

10.9 Worship in Light of Reconciliation

Reconciliation is a cause for worship and gratitude. Believers are called to praise God for His grace and mercy in restoring them to fellowship with Him.

- **Revelation 5:9**: "Thou art worthy…for thou wast slain, and hast redeemed us to God by thy blood out of every kindred, and tongue, and people, and nation."
- **Romans 11:36**: "For of him, and through him, and to him, are all things: to whom be glory for ever. Amen."

The work of reconciliation will be celebrated for all eternity as believers worship the Lamb who made peace through His blood.

Chapter 11: The Universal Scope of Atonement

11.1 The Extent of the Atonement

One of the most profound aspects of the atonement is its universal scope. The death of Christ has implications not only for individuals but also for humanity as a whole and even the created order. The breadth of the atonement demonstrates God's desire to redeem, restore, and reconcile all things to Himself.

- **John 3:16**: "For God so loved the world, that he gave his only begotten Son, that whosoever believeth in him should not perish, but have everlasting life."
- **1 John 2:2**: "And he is the propitiation for our sins: and not for ours only, but also for the sins of the whole world."

The atonement is sufficient for all humanity, but its application is limited to those who place their faith in Christ.

11.2 Christ's Death for All Humanity

The Bible repeatedly affirms that Christ's atonement is for the benefit of all people, regardless of nationality, ethnicity, or social status.

- **1 Timothy 2:5–6**: "For there is one God, and one mediator between God and men, the man Christ Jesus; who gave himself a ransom for all, to be testified in due time."
- **Titus 2:11**: "For the grace of God that bringeth salvation hath appeared to all men."

The inclusivity of the atonement reflects God's heart for the world and His desire that all would come to repentance (2 Peter 3:9).

11.3 Limited Atonement vs. Universal Atonement

The question of whether the atonement is limited or universal has been a topic of theological debate. While the atonement is sufficient for all, its efficacy applies only to those who believe.

- **Limited Atonement**: This view, often associated with Calvinism, argues that Christ died specifically for the elect, ensuring their salvation.
    - **Matthew 1:21**: "And she shall bring forth a son, and thou shalt call his name Jesus: for he shall save his people from their sins."
    - **John 10:15**: "I lay down my life for the sheep."
- **Universal Atonement**: This view, often associated with Arminianism, holds that Christ's death was for all people, offering salvation to everyone who believes.

- **1 John 2:2**: "And he is the propitiation for our sins: and not for ours only, but also for the sins of the whole world."
- **2 Corinthians 5:14–15**: "For the love of Christ constraineth us; because we thus judge, that if one died for all, then were all dead: and that he died for all, that they which live should not henceforth live unto themselves, but unto him which died for them, and rose again."

Regardless of the theological perspective, both views affirm the necessity of faith for salvation.

11.4 The Cosmic Scope of Atonement

The effects of the atonement extend beyond humanity to the entire creation, which has been subjected to corruption because of sin. Christ's death and resurrection are the means by which God will restore the universe to its intended state.

- **Colossians 1:19–20**: "For it pleased the Father that in him should all fulness dwell; and, having made peace through the blood of his cross, by him to reconcile all things unto himself."
- **Romans 8:21–22**: "Because the creature itself also shall be delivered from the bondage of corruption into the glorious liberty of the children of God. For we know that the whole creation groaneth and travaileth in pain together until now."

The atonement provides the foundation for the new heaven and new earth promised in Revelation 21:1.

11.5 The Inclusivity of the Gospel

The atonement demonstrates that salvation is available to all who believe, regardless of background, ethnicity, or social status.

- **Galatians 3:28**: "There is neither Jew nor Greek, there is neither bond nor free, there is neither male nor female: for ye are all one in Christ Jesus."
- **Revelation 5:9**: "Thou art worthy to take the book, and to open the seals thereof: for thou wast slain, and hast redeemed us to God by thy blood out of every kindred, and tongue, and people, and nation."

This inclusivity reflects the heart of God, who desires to bring people from every tribe and nation into His kingdom.

11.6 The Atonement and Evangelism

The universal scope of the atonement compels believers to share the gospel with the world. The message of reconciliation through Christ is entrusted to the church, which is called to proclaim it to all people.

- **2 Corinthians 5:18–20**: "And hath given to us the ministry of reconciliation… Now then we are

ambassadors for Christ, as though God did beseech you by us: we pray you in Christ's stead, be ye reconciled to God."
- **Matthew 28:19–20**: The Great Commission commands believers to "Go ye therefore, and teach all nations."

Evangelism is not optional but a responsibility that flows from the universal scope of Christ's atonement.

11.7 The Future Fulfillment of Atonement

The ultimate fulfillment of the atonement will be realized when Christ returns and establishes His eternal kingdom. At that time, all things will be fully reconciled to God, and His glory will fill the earth.

- **Revelation 21:3–4**: "And I heard a great voice out of heaven saying, Behold, the tabernacle of God is with men, and he will dwell with them, and they shall be his people, and God himself shall be with them, and be their God. And God shall wipe away all tears from their eyes; and there shall be no more death, neither sorrow, nor crying, neither shall there be any more pain: for the former things are passed away."
- **Philippians 2:10–11**: "That at the name of Jesus every knee should bow, of things in heaven, and things in earth, and things under the earth; and that every tongue should confess that Jesus Christ is Lord, to the glory of God the Father."

11.8 Worship in Light of the Universal Atonement

The universal scope of the atonement inspires worship and gratitude, as believers from every nation praise God for His redemptive work.

- **Psalm 96:3**: "Declare his glory among the heathen, his wonders among all people."
- **Revelation 7:9–10**: "After this I beheld, and, lo, a great multitude, which no man could number, of all nations, and kindreds, and people, and tongues, stood before the throne, and before the Lamb, clothed with white robes, and palms in their hands; and cried with a loud voice, saying, Salvation to our God which sitteth upon the throne, and unto the Lamb."

Chapter 12: Atonement and the Kingdom of God

12.1 The Kingdom of God: An Overview

The Kingdom of God is central to the biblical narrative, representing God's reign over all creation. The atonement of Christ is the means by which the Kingdom of God is established and expanded, reconciling humanity and creation to the rightful rule of God.

- **Mark 1:15**: Jesus proclaimed, "The time is fulfilled, and the kingdom of God is at hand: repent ye, and believe the gospel."
- **Definition**: The Kingdom of God refers to God's sovereign rule over His people, His purposes, and all creation. It is both a present reality and a future hope.

The atonement is essential to the Kingdom because it addresses the fundamental problem of sin, which separates humanity from God and undermines His reign.

12.2 The Inauguration of the Kingdom

The atonement marked the inauguration of the Kingdom of God. Through His death and resurrection, Jesus defeated the powers of sin, death, and Satan, reclaiming authority over creation.

- **Colossians 1:13–14**: "Who hath delivered us from the power of darkness, and hath translated us into the kingdom of his dear Son: in whom we have redemption through his blood, even the forgiveness of sins."
- **1 Corinthians 15:25**: "For he must reign, till he hath put all enemies under his feet."

The cross and resurrection are the decisive events through which God's reign was established in a new and transformative way.

12.3 The Kingdom as Redemption and Restoration

The atonement not only redeems individuals but also restores the created order. The Kingdom of God brings healing to what was broken by sin.

- **Isaiah 61:1–2**: This prophecy, fulfilled in Christ, describes the redemptive mission of the Messiah: "The Spirit of the Lord God is upon me…to bind up the brokenhearted, to proclaim liberty to the captives, and the opening of the prison to them that are bound."
- **Romans 8:21**: "Because the creature itself also shall be delivered from the bondage of corruption into the glorious liberty of the children of God."

The atonement sets the stage for the ultimate renewal of all things, including the physical creation.

12.4 The Kingdom Manifested in the Church

The church is the primary manifestation of the Kingdom of God on earth, living as a redeemed community that proclaims and embodies the gospel.

- **Ephesians 2:19–22**: Believers are described as "fellowcitizens with the saints, and of the household of God," being built into a holy temple for the Lord.
- **Matthew 16:18–19**: Jesus declared, "Upon this rock I will build my church; and the gates of hell shall not prevail against it." The church is commissioned to advance the Kingdom by proclaiming the gospel and living in obedience to Christ.

The atonement unites believers into one body, empowering them to carry out the mission of the Kingdom.

12.5 The Kingdom's Ethical Implications

The atonement transforms the lives of believers, enabling them to live according to the values of the Kingdom of God. These values include love, humility, and justice.

- **Romans 12:1–2**: Paul urges believers to live as a "living sacrifice," reflecting the transformative power of the atonement.
- **Matthew 5:3–10**: The Beatitudes outline the character of Kingdom citizens, such as being merciful, pure in heart, and peacemakers.

The Kingdom ethic is rooted in the atonement, which provides both the example and the power to live a holy life.

12.6 The Future Fulfillment of the Kingdom

While the Kingdom of God is already present through the work of Christ, it will be fully realized at His second coming. The atonement guarantees this future fulfillment.

- **Revelation 11:15**: "The kingdoms of this world are become the kingdoms of our Lord, and of his Christ; and he shall reign for ever and ever."
- **1 Corinthians 15:24–26**: Paul describes the consummation of the Kingdom: "Then cometh the end, when he shall have delivered up the kingdom to God, even the Father; when he shall have put down all rule and all authority and power. For he must reign, till he hath put all enemies under his feet."

At this time, all things will be fully reconciled to God, and His reign will be complete.

12.7 The Role of the Atonement in the Kingdom's Consummation

The atonement is central to the final realization of the Kingdom. By addressing the problem of sin, Christ's work ensures the ultimate restoration of creation and the eternal reign of God.

- **Revelation 21:3–4**: "And I heard a great voice out of heaven saying, Behold, the tabernacle of God is with men, and he will dwell with them, and they shall be his people, and God himself shall be with them, and be their God. And God shall wipe away all tears from their eyes; and there shall be no more death, neither sorrow, nor crying, neither shall there be any more pain."
- **Philippians 2:10–11**: "That at the name of Jesus every knee should bow… and that every tongue should confess that Jesus Christ is Lord, to the glory of God the Father."

The atonement secures the complete victory of the Kingdom, where sin and death will be no more.

12.8 The Worship of the King

The atonement establishes Christ as the rightful King of the universe, worthy of eternal worship and adoration.

- **Revelation 5:12–13**: "Worthy is the Lamb that was slain to receive power, and riches, and

wisdom, and strength, and honor, and glory, and blessing."
- **Psalm 22:27–28**: "All the ends of the world shall remember and turn unto the Lord... For the kingdom is the Lord's: and he is the governor among the nations."

Worship is the natural response to the atonement and the reality of God's reign.

Chapter 13: Eternal Worship of the Lamb

13.1 The Centrality of Christ in Eternal Worship

The atonement is not only the foundation of salvation but also the eternal focus of worship in heaven. The Lamb who was slain is exalted above all, and the redeemed will forever glorify Him for His sacrificial love and victory over sin.

- **Revelation 5:12–13**: "Worthy is the Lamb that was slain to receive power, and riches, and wisdom, and strength, and honor, and glory, and blessing. And every creature… heard I saying, Blessing, and honor, and glory, and power, be unto him that sitteth upon the throne, and unto the Lamb for ever and ever."
- **Revelation 7:9–10**: The multitude of the redeemed cry out, "Salvation to our God which sitteth upon the throne, and unto the Lamb."

Eternal worship centers on Christ because His atonement reveals the depth of God's love, the perfection of His justice, and the glory of His grace.

13.2 The Song of the Redeemed

Throughout Scripture, worship is often expressed through song, and in eternity, the atonement will inspire a new and everlasting song of praise.

- **Revelation 5:9**: "And they sung a new song, saying, Thou art worthy to take the book, and to open the seals thereof: for thou wast slain, and hast redeemed us to God by thy blood out of every kindred, and tongue, and people, and nation."
- **Psalm 40:3**: "And he hath put a new song in my mouth, even praise unto our God: many shall see it, and fear, and shall trust in the Lord."

The "new song" reflects the joy, gratitude, and awe of those who have experienced the saving power of the Lamb.

13.3 The Everlasting Impact of the Atonement

The significance of the atonement will never fade because it reveals the eternal character of God and His redemptive purpose for creation.

- **Ephesians 2:7**: "That in the ages to come he might shew the exceeding riches of his grace in his kindness toward us through Christ Jesus."
- **1 Peter 1:18–19**: The atonement is described as precious and eternal: "Ye were not redeemed with corruptible things…but with the precious

blood of Christ, as of a lamb without blemish and without spot."

The cross is not merely a historical event but an eternal revelation of God's glory, worthy of endless reflection and praise.

13.4 Worship as the Fulfillment of the Atonement

The ultimate purpose of the atonement is to bring humanity into a restored relationship with God, resulting in eternal worship and communion with Him.

- **John 4:23–24**: "The hour cometh, and now is, when the true worshippers shall worship the Father in spirit and in truth: for the Father seeketh such to worship him."
- **Revelation 21:3**: "Behold, the tabernacle of God is with men, and he will dwell with them, and they shall be his people, and God himself shall be with them, and be their God."

The atonement makes it possible for believers to worship God in His presence, free from the barriers of sin and death.

13.5 The Role of the Lamb in God's Eternal Kingdom

In the eternal Kingdom of God, Christ as the Lamb is not only the object of worship but also the source of life, light, and joy.

- **Revelation 21:22–23**: "And I saw no temple therein: for the Lord God Almighty and the Lamb are the temple of it. And the city had no need of the sun, neither of the moon, to shine in it: for the glory of God did lighten it, and the Lamb is the light thereof."
- **Revelation 22:1–3**: "And he shewed me a pure river of water of life, clear as crystal, proceeding out of the throne of God and of the Lamb... And there shall be no more curse: but the throne of God and of the Lamb shall be in it; and his servants shall serve him."

The Lamb remains central to the eternal life of the redeemed, symbolizing the completion of God's redemptive plan.

13.6 The Gathering of the Nations

The atonement has a global impact, and in eternity, people from every nation, tribe, and language will gather to worship the Lamb.

- **Isaiah 66:18**: "It shall come, that I will gather all nations and tongues; and they shall come, and see my glory."
- **Revelation 7:9**: The multitude of worshipers includes "all nations, and kindreds, and people, and tongues," united in praise.

This global worship reflects the inclusivity of the atonement and the glory of God's redemptive purpose.

13.7 Eternal Gratitude for the Atonement

The atonement will inspire eternal gratitude among the redeemed, who will forever marvel at the grace and love of God.

- **Psalm 103:1–4**: "Bless the Lord, O my soul: and all that is within me, bless his holy name. Bless the Lord, O my soul, and forget not all his benefits: who forgiveth all thine iniquities; who healeth all thy diseases; who redeemeth thy life from destruction."
- **2 Corinthians 9:15**: "Thanks be unto God for his unspeakable gift."

Eternal worship is the believer's ultimate response to the unspeakable gift of the atonement.

13.8 The Eternal Glory of the Lamb

The Lamb will be exalted forever, and His glory will fill the new heaven and earth.

- **Revelation 5:13**: "And every creature which is in heaven, and on the earth, and under the earth, and such as are in the sea, and all that are in them, heard I saying, Blessing, and honor, and glory, and power, be unto him that sitteth upon the throne, and unto the Lamb for ever and ever."
- **Philippians 2:10–11**: "That at the name of Jesus every knee should bow… and that every tongue

should confess that Jesus Christ is Lord, to the glory of God the Father."

The eternal glory of the Lamb reflects the infinite worth of His sacrifice and the magnitude of God's redemptive plan.

Conclusion

The atonement is the cornerstone of God's redemptive work, securing forgiveness, reconciliation, and eternal life for humanity. It is through the blood of Christ that believers are justified, sanctified, and glorified, and it is through His atonement that all creation will be restored.

As the Lamb of God, Jesus will forever be exalted in worship. The cross, the resurrection, and the eternal reign of Christ reveal the depth of God's love, the perfection of His justice, and the glory of His grace. In eternity, the redeemed will join with all creation to proclaim:

"Worthy is the Lamb that was slain!"

Made in the USA
Columbia, SC
23 February 2025